CIVIL TWILIGHT

Crab Orchard Series in Poetry
Editor's Selection

Civil Twilight

CYNTHIA HUNTINGTON

Crab Orchard Review & Southern Illinois University Press/ Carbondale

Southern Illinois University Press
www.siupress.com

Printed in the United States of America

27 26 25 24 4 3 2 1

Cover illustration: MK Beach Sky by MK Beach. Image has been cropped.

The Crab Orchard Series in Poetry is a joint publishing venture of Southern Illinois University Press and *Crab Orchard Review*. This series has been made possible by the generous support of the Office of the President of Southern Illinois University; the Office of the Vice Chancellor for Academic Affairs and Provost; and the School of Literature, Writing, and Digital Humanities in the College of Liberal Arts at Southern Illinois University Carbondale.

Editor of the Crab Orchard Series in Poetry: Allison Joseph
Jon Tribble, series founder and editor, 1998–2019

Library of Congress Cataloging-in-Publication Data

Names: Huntington, Cynthia, 1951– author.
Title: Civil twilight / Cynthia Huntington.
Identifiers: LCCN 2023026966 (print) | LCCN 2023026967 (ebook) | ISBN 9780809339303 (paperback) | ISBN 9780809339310 (ebook)
Subjects: LCGFT: Poetry.
Classification: LCC PS3558.U517 C58 2024 (print) | LCC PS3558.U517 (ebook) | DDC 811/.54—dc23/eng/20230616
LC record available at https://lccn.loc.gov/2023026966
LC ebook record available at https://lccn.loc.gov/2023026967

Printed on recycled paper ♲

Southern Illinois University System

CONTENTS

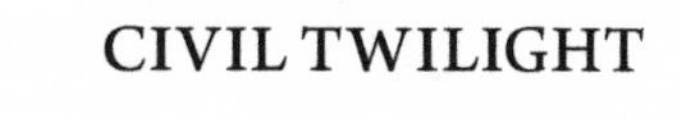

CIVIL TWILIGHT

HARD FROST

How do you like this morning, frozen dandelion?
Shriveled and black-fringed, yet you seem more distinct—
dilly-toothed rosette, green-darkening wraith.
My old cat glowers on the doorstep, shrinks back.
He's saying it's time for fires.
And what of that blue jay, whose loud complaint
startles the dreaming maple to throw up her arms,
flustering leaves down in accolade, rave
to his magnitude? What he wants wants wants
is to live, of course, and yes he loves the world
as well. He is a blue prince among the colors of fire.
Bright as a break in clouds, he struts and glares.
Hello. Come closer please. One dazzled fly
creaking to life among the blackened stalks.

PART ONE: *Snow*

If this were the beginning of a poem, he would have called the thing he felt inside him the silence of snow.

—*Snow,* Orhan Pamuk

AFTER A LINE BY TRANSTROMER

Turn down the lights
and let dusk fill the window glass,
pour whiskey in a cup and drink
in honor of the day: so long,
nice knowing/not-knowing
you. The low sky gleams.

Down the hall the composer is recording
ambient sound, and the amplified hum
inside a metal lampshade, how it bends the air,
which even inside a room is always moving.
Silence, like emptiness, only an idea.

Across the road, beside the frozen lake,
the red house wakes and turns on its lights.
Smoke from the chimney,
lit by the sun's last angle, sighs upward—
for a few moments somehow brighter than the sky,
then not. The sky is a lake. *The lake is a window*
into the earth. The window is a mirror,
then a lens closing.

A fluttering like birds,
the heat comes up in the furnace.
Then footsteps, someone walking on my ceiling,
someone living in the air above.
I'm living in this air below,
alone, but nearby.
Hearing them, so not alone.
But alone. The glass is dark now
and headlights flick on in the sky,
no, they're winding down the hill.
Behind each light a face
staring into the dark
out of the other dark.

NOW THAT I AM IN FINLAND AND CAN THINK

I think of dark matter, which is not,
after all, dark, but transparent.
Leaving us in the dark, so to speak.
I think of dark matter because it's dark here,
November in this northern latitude
when the world shrinks down to a room,
a lamp, a disc of light cast on the table
at four o'clock when the world disappears.
But the dark is light to those who can see:
this I also was told, and in truth believe.
The material universe we know may be slight,
a mere one-digit fraction of the whole,
but we've cornered the market on information.
In fact, we are made of information:
an atom is not a thing. We are a motion, a phrase,
an unseen sway of forces in nonexistent spacetime.
Rotation. Revolution. All spin and shuffle,
counting one-two, one-two—one small step
out of the cradle endlessly toppling, we the incarnate
(meatified) create like mad a world of ones and zeros,
strange loops and melodies, circuits and links.

So, the Finnish tango and the Irish whiskey,
the migrating swans set down in a stubbled field,
and the bluing light, which is to say,
the lessening of light, that gathers now in hollows,
in small particles that circle like gnats,
the chill when landscape shivers,
ice on the lake reflecting sky, the water
dark inside its luminous skin.
Crystal fistfuls crushed to ooze.
All that, yet more: these uncalled-for delights,
like finding pistachio gelato at the truck stop
where we stopped for coffee after driving
dark woods, hours inside a private corridor

scraped by headlights' spotlit glow,
the limelight's candoluminescence.
The lights in the minimart shape a theater of glass
where bottles shine in cases,
refreshment to sustain a frame:
my loneliness and yours on display.

And out there
beyond these black windows, the nothing,
which is after all something,
lost to us who want everything. And it's there,
close your eyes and it's out there, almost in reach,
one-two, one-two, a chaos stamped in time,
and I've tried to be holy, but God likes me mad.
He's dark as hell and eats fire,
whole galaxies swirled down his throat,
as gold as burnt honey. I can't take his measure,
invisible structures that fill me, forms I kindle with being.
I can't dance at the dance hall. The dance is deep structure
learned in the body's depths, the couples circling on the snow
in boots and coats. Red skirts swirl, feet stamp,
each couple turning, turning as two, somber kaleidoscope
and the bodies held close; you must not smile
when you dance the tango, only crazy people smile,
it is a melancholy figure, less flare than smolder,
a composition tightly measured;
tandem bodies locked in twirl.
We're here for the duration, slant rotation.
Revolution put a spin on it, and yes it's true
that once we waited, dipped in nothing,
and a light from the beginning of time
was wandering the unmade universe, looking
for a body to rest upon, to save it from
oblivion, and found in our dense matter
a place to become.

It was like a Russian novel: everyone coming and going in the big room overlooking the lake, drifting into the kitchen for tea, then back to their rooms, or wrapping themselves in coats and scarves to hike out on the woods' trails, or up the road by the lake, then banging back inside, chattering, strewing boots and gloves and hats and snowy jackets in the cold entry hall.

Forbidden to walk out on the lake: thin ice with wet patches rising through. "But the men are out there fishing." "Yes, they know where to walk."

I lay on the sofa with my book. On the other side of a screen Ina was helping Louise decipher a bus schedule, speaking English, which is not the first language for either one, but Ina doesn't speak French, and no one speaks Finnish (except everyone who lives here—but we don't live here, we are guests.)

Cissy is playing some kind of gypsy music on a guitar she found leaned up in the closet, and Brandon and Dani are working on a sculpture with string and tags from teabags tacked to the wall, a model to sketch out an idea, and if they use wire instead of string for the next version, Nate says he can make it play music. Beautiful Clara is brooding on a floor cushion, sitting cross-legged with a drawing pad in her lap, staring out the window, adrift in a sadness known only to the beautiful young—that time when you first feel how vast your loneliness is, but still believe it can be healed.

Omar has taken the car into town, along with our liquor orders. Someone is heating a curry in the kitchen. It smells . . . out of place . . . in this cold light, but good. I'm thinking I didn't come here for company, I have work to do, but my room is cold, even with a blanket over my lap, and I like it here in the commons after all, falling into my book and surfacing again.

Now I remember I didn't go out that day because I had burned my foot—an accident involving a pan of hot chicken broth that spilled and splashed up and clung to my skin, burned deep through layers, and I was lying on the sofa with my leg propped on pillows, and the foot throbbed and was too swollen for a shoe. That week of wool socks over bandages, and a size 13 slipper, also found in the closet, and I was waiting with some small urgency for Omar to return and bring my Irish whiskey. And it wasn't a Russian novel at all, though one does require an invalid, and a house party, but no one was arguing or about to lose their estate, so no . . .

Finally I pulled a blanket up over my shoulders and dozed. It was that kind of day. Cozy, like sleeping in the back of the car, driving home on a winter night, my parents talking in the front seat about nothing interesting, and tucking my head down in my coat—the cold outside and the musty heater and the car's rolling motion along the two-lane road, carried safe. When I woke up Dani was showing slides projected on the wall. It was dark, though still afternoon, and Omar had returned and everyone was drinking and talking softly and my bottle sat on the table beside my hand.

Can I call it a dream if it was real? Maybe a small fever attended the burn, a drowsy waking in which I found myself remembering the day even as it was happening, so that I seemed to be in two lives at once, a kind of wholeness. no less true for being imagined. Not every dream is an illusion. And imagination is a place: I remember being there.

COMMUNITY CENTER YOGA

Each is not every. Every is not all.
The eager voice in my mind,
hurrying to save the dream on cusp of waking.
It's that voice that drives the dream away,
the voice of explaining,
because the voice inside the dream
can't know the dream it is inside.

I wake again in the exercise studio,
cold, because the power went out last night
and zero skies froze the heights of the open ceiling,
steel trusses buttressing the gymnasium floor above.

I can hear them upstairs running, feet pounding the floor.
Again I forgot my mat and need to unroll a common one,
wipe it with sanitizer and hope for the best.
A woman dressed for yoga in Bermuda shorts
and argyle socks turns sideways as the light
from a high window slices her face.
"I'm leaving on my shoes," she says; "this floor is ice."
A girl pulls a blanket over her head. That girl,
I saw her here last week. Long brown hair,
the face of a child. She barely tried the poses,
just sat on the floor, gazing upward,
making shapes in the air with her hands.

Now we are to breathe, and lift our hearts (physical)
toward our upraised arms; we are to open,
to bend and close, only as we feel moved
or able, to do only so much as is right.

By the water fountain I saw a man I knew years ago.
The editor of a literary press, retired now,
thirty pounds heavier and pale.
I didn't recognize him until he spoke.
And now I remember that he was fired,
or "replaced," from that job. What since?
Once you are "replaced," where are you placed?

The mirror along the front wall shows the room in reverse.
I can't see the teacher from where I'm standing,
so I follow the ones who can. Facing ahead,
I watch the back of the room. The girl has slipped her hand
inside the waistband of her shorts, rubbing herself
gently, with a look of content, her lips relaxed,
jaw slack, her eyes far seeing. Now we stand up
and need to place blocks under our hands,
bending sideways, one arm sweeping a slow arc
across and back, describing a breath.

In the dream a nail had been driven through my ankle,
and it pulled at the skin, ripping at the edges,
and scraping bone when I moved.
A man held my foot in his hand,
cradling it, and teased out the nail.
It was as easy as pulling a hair from a sweater,
but I had been afraid.

The teacher's blonde hair falls across her face
in one swoop, veiling her, then parts when she turns,
and there she is again. Someone is walking back and forth
along the back wall, working out a cramp maybe,
or nursing some sore part,
walking slowly, not looking at anyone.

We're all on our knees, folded in child pose,
our foreheads down; the room looks like a mosque.
I stepped on a prayer rug once
in the night market in Kantagora.
I thought it was a welcome mat outside the little stall
—there was nearly a scene, settled with five naira.
A man starts grunting, roars, some heads turn,
the woman beside him touches his shoulder
and he settles. The sun squares have shifted
across the floor, my stomach rumbles,
and a woman in a red sweatshirt
begins rolling up her mat, "I have to go,"
pointing to the clock, and the door opens,
to a bubble of voices in the hall, closes again;
we wait in the quiet a few more minutes;
my bad shoulder is beginning to ache.

ONE LAMP IN A DOORWAY AND ONE DOWN THE VALLEY

Snow sweeps down the road,
blown sideways and rolling up in thick flakes.
My boots stamp fresh prints
that fill with snow and are brushed by wind.
How quickly everything falls away
and is lost—not changed but covered over.
A few house lights shimmer past the trees,
the branches' jigsaw scores the low sky.
In a neighbor's dooryard wild turkeys
purr and cluck, milling the bare-swept ground
where a woman has thrown down corn.
Coins to the beggar. Rice in the monk's bowl.
If that's what love is, it's too little,
though maybe too much to hope for.

Lights switch on in the hills,
and across the river a line of headlights
tracks in formation across the sky. Two stars
blink on and off as clouds part then close again.
They spend it all, the stars that is, in being.
I'm down here in the earth, where snow is falling,
winnowing through the tall hemlocks. Down the road:
one lamp in a doorway, and another down the valley,
shining through an open barn.

AT THE DEATH HOUSE

Morning talk in the kitchen, no one slept.
People coming in and going out,
the coffee pot emptied, filled again.

"He wanted to kiss Grandpa goodbye.
OK, I said, you go on in there before the man comes."

Then my hand shook and the bottle spilled
—dull bile-green pills flew skidding
across the linoleum floor. Pick them up
one by one and blow the dust away,
count them back into the bottle for hospice to collect.

"She didn't want to let his body go;
she kept saying, 'Don't you take him.'"

"Shane called, wants to know is Ronny coming in to work. I said,
His father died nine hours ago—you think he's coming to work?"

Stepping out into the clean cold,
the morning is silver, it rings when you touch it.
Snow has blown all over the road
and after all the plows' work through the night,
I can't make out any lanes.
Mailboxes bob on cresting waves
above snowfields that reach all the way to Canada.

"Where are you going?"
"To the store. People have to eat."
"Why?" she said.

SPIKE

This icicle descending from the eave over the window
beside the bed where I lie all day and watch it melt
and freeze, and drip in sun and freeze again,
growing long and thin, a channel for snowmelt,
a dagger aimed at the hard-frozen earth,
endures. I no longer believe it will ever disappear,
dissolve into water and bless the grass.
I no longer believe it is water, like the water in my flesh.
I no longer believe in mercy, at the end of time is ice
and stars' fires gone out; in separate rooms we watch
through glass the end. Ice drips like venom from a fang,
last bead of morphine stopping breath. One icicle, bending light,
hangs shining. Cold sky with one bird flying.

SHELTER

A snow cave is warm
and even an empty church
at night when the lights are doused
will keep out the cold and the wind,
and the snow falling steady
in a silence that is not life.
Make a tent of cardboard
piled and lapped like shingles, or crawl in
among pine branches you've pulled down.
Birds love the hemlocks,
mice an abandoned barn.
Whatever will keep off the sky
that calls you back with stars.
Here, the smallest flame is home.
You wish to remain here in the earth,
to sleep covered, hidden,
under all that vast. You do.

FIREWOOD

This morning's clean cold air,
I wrap my hands under my forearms,
outside chatting with a neighbor delivering firewood.
His grandmother lived on this road
but he doesn't remember my house.
His son lives in the next town over;
I tell him mine's overseas.
I think he thinks I'm someone else.
When I hand him the check
he takes it gravely, folds it twice,
and tucks it in his shirt pocket under his jacket.
A working man making a good living,
he's cheerful today. New Carhartt's,
new gloves (it's two days past Christmas),
newish truck with his name painted on the side,
a nice design of pine trees for a logo.
The wood's a sideline; he's a mason and carpenter.
He reminds me of my uncles when I was young.
Handsome, gentle men who worked with their hands
and strong backs, who could make things
and fix them. That world I was raised to forget.
My father was ashamed, my mother afraid
of being poor and nobody. Lonely then
moving on from there, they seemed to swim
inside themselves like carp in a tank.
He backs the truck up to the bulkhead,
tips the load. Tumbling crash of logs
on frozen ground. He says, "Get that covered
soon as you can, that wood is good and dry."
I reach to shake his hand
and he says, "Hey, a hug for New Year's."
Small against him, the good scent of a man
folds me in childhood's safety.
A young man, thirty years my junior,
sees an old woman alone.

RIVER ROAD

Now I'm driving down the valley in first light,
repeating the names of God as I steer through curves
and over inclines, praise on my lips—not in vain repetition,
as Matthew says of the heathens, and Jesus of the hypocrites,
who live piling merit up on earth, but inside the continuing
instant of prayer that is an offering of self to the moment.
This here and now always: God, God . . .
I don't want to sleep through my life but I do,
my mind running on with thoughts for tomorrow,
laying up treasures in my imagination.
The thermometer inches toward double digits.
The sky is pale, trailing white scrolls of cloud.
Now the train rises beyond the trees,
moving down the river, white with fresh snow.
A brushstroke and a painted line, then another.
The train pulling slow, hauling logs strapped and trussed,
trees of the Great North Woods, *Grand Bois du Nord*.
Boxcar, flatcar, flatline, blacktop; meanwhile the traffic
drifts north and south. Starlings, shabby and glistening,
brood in a dawn-wet tree—what knowledge in the small
bird's head, its memory of light and shifting currents?
They read the earth's ancestral signs, how light rides
the river, the opening among trees, a slash of white,
a snow path, ice. The river makes a clearing. Train tracks
slice into earth; crushed stone and steel nudge bedrock base.
We move along the surface of a rock thrown out in space,
in each of us a world that keeps us from the world.
The train paces me, heading south, disappears behind trees

and emerges at the bend. We must never lose
the spirit of repetition, Suzuki Roshi said, the delicious
mystery of practice, how things are done again,
the same but changed. Creation's whole. I think I know
what's next, and I do: just past the hairpin turn
a green pickup floats upended in ice, its rear gate
pointed to the sky. The driver skidded off the road
and swam to shore; it hangs there, frozen in till spring.
Wild turkeys congress on the center line, all fuss and fluster:
pray for them. God, God, Abba, Father, Lord . . .
I'm moving with everything that moves, in praise,
as everything must praise these astonishing, unlikely
appearances of wave and current, the train's engine
lit up inside, glowing like a coal, red fire of morning
planted in the heart of the thing, the driver awake
at the controls, the track laid down ahead and behind,
and these intersecting planes carrying motion, trees
moving through trees, water flowing under ice. How the river
carves a shore, a place of pause where woods stand back,
a swath of light among the pressing wild.
A span, a distance, a division among parts—white highway,
thread of light we follow, riding on iron and oil, turning time
inside out, in fear and trembling, burning ancient carbon,
star particles scattered, billions of stellar sparks.
Dread this sun now quickening.

PART TWO: *Civil Twilight*

Now I will dance you the War, which you did not prevent and for which you are responsible.

—Vaslav Nijinsky

DEMOLITION

No wound without an afterlife:
a length of clothesline looped on a nail
driven into a grey-shingled wall
commemorates a moment's work, a blow.

The carpenter and the electrician
are arguing in the courtyard.
The radio's cranked high, tuned to chaos,
the elements of harmony thrown in heap
along with snarl of saw and thud of hammer,
the squeal of pried boards and the high
and grating slide into the dumpster.

Morning's blue air scatters light, salt on my eyelids
heavy, slight. They've driven the garden down
to ash and stone, and overrun
this scrap of lawn surveyed by windows.
An empty space, a place long disregarded,
that left a zone of quiet between lives.

I stand behind a wall,
inside a room, beside a window,
rooting clippings from the ruined ivy in a jar.
Green naked unstalked shoot reborn.
The full-leafed lilac, spared beyond the margin,
stirs with shimmer, leaf and flash.

Now fluidly the purple gleam
that flickers in the branch resolves
to siege of grackles, rabble of the underworld.
Their sleek heads baptized in some iridescent oil,
they gape their beaks and bow.

Their cries' hot wire snarl and squawk
ground under by machines, they speak
as the dead must speak, in gestures,
dumb show under din.

THE MEEK SHALL EAT OUR DUST

The first people came in Chevrolets. Some had canoes strapped to their roof racks, with paddles set crosswise, for that they were holy. Their children had sticky hands, and the middle girl, who was carsick, vomited frequently. The brothers quarreled and swatted each other, like brothers in the Bible, their mother said. The parents smoked in the front seat and tipped their ashes out the windows. Behind them, forest fires raged. Just past the mountains the car broke down, and there by the road they waited. An angel came and bid them to keep faith and know that they were not forgotten. This heartened them and they hoped that a tow truck had been called, as they were hot and weary, and without recourse for the car was still broke down. As they sat there by the roadside, faithful in sorrow, a Chrysler sailed past. A powder-blue convertible with clean whitewalls and silvery chrome, radio thumping *a-wimeweh a-wimeweh* from state-of-the-art speakers. Froth of music, and chiffon scarves ruffling in the breeze. Look quick: those are our ancestors, lost in clouds of road dust gasoline alley glory. As for that family stranded by the roadside, who loved each other and were patient in suffering, they have not been heard of since.

APRIL PASTORAL

The American landscape painting of our time
should be sketched in a smear from a moving car.
The American landscape of our time is a parking lot,
arrested engines hiring space by the hour,
and we all agree we don't like it much here today,
trapped in this conurban sprawl—no, we'd rather be in the city,
but not that city that went underwater, or caught
on that coastline with flames running down from the hills,
or any city at war, and please God, not stranded in some sector
where natural disaster, terror conspiracy, or technical failure
has cut off the lights. One cell at a time, one cell at a time,
words are dissolving in melting terraces, lines
fallen free of history. Drive on.
News streams live feed from holiday gridlock
(roadblock, logjam, bottleneck, backup),
and helicopters scan delays, lifted above the snarl
of expressways, looking down over rooftops,
and down on the nest of the peregrine falcons
baffled into high-rise lodgings, glimpsed here clasping
claws in air, grappling to couple among the silver,
arcing spans. That gleam on glass, reflection's
weak gesture waves. Somebody locked the trees out;
they fumble the frames as if they remembered us.
This world is printed in our bones. Stones drink sun.
Today the blue light on the hills, engenderer of birds and green,
the red-tail's wing along the river vein. One sky at a time,
one sky at a time, the bird says, winging, wheeling,
and now is the time before time, now the fractal
ice melt split—land howls in storm winds, spring and all
April's dementia uncovering scars, and the downed power line

lies in the road unstrung, convulsing, sputtering code, signing:
who am I? who am I? thrashing with holy fit on fire,
the branch not consumed. No peace, no peace, and the seed
splits out of itself once, once again, now again,
and in every quake are signals and portents,
the voice out of air uproaring: pick up if you're there.

MUD SEASON

The swamp could not invent the wheel:
you need a stable surface to proceed.
An army likes a road where nothing grows.
Lay down a highway called philosophy
and I will drive and point out sites
along the way, remarking landmarks
with their mottoes granite-ground.
Land must be hard to take a mark.
There will be collisions, losses,
one more casual fatality. We'll see
what rises then, what traffic overcomes.

They say that if a thousand soldiers march in step
across a bridge, the bridge will fall.
You can't have things too uniform. Reject
drumbeat monotony. Force multiplies potential
exponentially, it's the give in things,
the bounce, small matter's play, that saves.
So ask more questions, kids; it'll help
throw off the beat, break up the reverb,
which, we have determined, scuppers all.
Two cheers for chaos! We amass
hypotheses, though stonerock fall.

CONVERSION METRIC

Rome gave us the standing army. Hell to pay
for the conquered, and empire paid for itself.
My people were out throwing stones at barricades,
manning the ramparts with their bodies.
Lag in technology, or scarcity of resource?
A pillar of fire, a column of smoke,
the tyrant's face on the money.
I was squatted on a trash heap,
beating clay into potsherds.
Vermin and worms, loathsome germs:
I would not take food from your hands
or bow down to your lizard god.

If only we'd had horses! Oh, then you'd see us ride,
come charging down upon your city gates!
Your walls no refuge then, but trap,
you'd taste our rage, our might.
Our torches brandished high, we'd fly,
and flee with bloody prize.

Napoleon's march outmarched itself;
an army too big to feed
ate up the land and starved. How far is far?
The measure mile derives from mill:
one thousand paces of a Roman soldier.
Queen Victoria traded meter for furlong,
meaning the long side of an acre,
what a yoke of oxen could plow in a day
when the sun did not set on her domain.
We measure empire in bodies:
a journey is a day, a league an hour,

and march is measure to body's mortal bound.
It's down to the farmer, the soldier, the serf,
to every conscript the dirty work,
the trudge, the mire, the drear campaign.
Then render to Caesar the fat of the land.
Keep the change.

DACIA

The castle belongs to the people now; no one can live there.
A footpath leads up to the lookout and the public toilets beyond:
you've learned to carry tissues. The Roma watch you
with hard eyes; they are hated and feared. You fear them, too,
a kind of hate. Sinister glamour, the knife tucked in a shawl.
Bodies asleep beside stone walls at the train station.
Black plums in a white paper bag. Grey crumbling high-rise
offices the state built, pocked concrete blocking sky.
The rebels waited on the mountain for help that never came.
Its white peak gazes down on cars that labor up the pass
to the ski hotel, the road turning, snaking on itself.
The tyrant's face was on the money and in public meeting places.
We're spending the new money in millions; a small beer
costs six figures. But up in the fortified city, for centuries
threat was an army on foot. Invasion, incursion, insurgency.
Treachery, reprieve. Watch out for movement in the trees.
Under the trees. Look for birds flying up in the leaves.
The defender of homeland a famous murderer of Turks,
a plaque marks his house. Up from under, down from above.
A horse drags a plow through a rocky field. A Roman fountain
sits empty in the square where sparrows bathe their fleas in dust.
The monastery closed at four and we missed seeing the mosaics.

HOW TO READ AMERICAN HISTORY, CHAPTER FOUR

Now we are safe in Connecticut, we feel
more grey than blue. More red than dead,
our aim less true. First world forgot,
we drive our carts across the bones
of all the lost. Drive on, steer north,
expressway opens, life replacing life,
and projects' view of generations cast abroad.
This waste of outskirts, big box stores,
electric warehouse wasteland desert, swept
by air-bridged harbor, intestate, for miles unhoused.
Let dead rest there, let grieving stand.
In fact nowadays we can't be giving land
in acres up to cemeteries. Angel stones,
those Jesus aviaries. Signs out of time,
graffiti sings: *God fuck. Forgeve. Maria diarrhea . . .*
Miles carry on old mother tongue,
read nightmare blues of grammar grunt and moan,
the song where stones stud riverbed like stars:
step onward counting: One. One. One.
The city lies behind us fuming, haze o'erhanging,
dream of Jeannie, fragile air gust borne
in shaft contagion vapor there.
Cholera emptied young Isaac out:
gone into death, no more to lie
his feet behind the stove, no more to read
by lamplight, moving lips in prayer
to sound out words by shape, and yet still come
the boats, and each like souls raised wing,
sailed full. Each always now forever
still arriving.

LATE TENEMENT, 1974

After the codes they opened the stairwells,
changed out wood for stone and tiled the entry,
tinned the ceilings, bronzed the letterboxes.

It was all I could ask for:
three rooms, three windows, one escape.
The bathroom squeezed into a corner
carved out from the kitchen—
better than the shared hall toilets
that replaced the courtyard privies of original design.
Heat coming up the pipes, bare, burn to touch.
Don't touch.

Glass shatter air shaft echo night fight alley:
gangs and street rats, thugs and hoods.
Rosa next door, her mother and her aunt,
cooking together, all day carried pots down the hall.
Sally with his pigeons on the roof, *coo-roo.*
Sunday Social Club for men, card tables
set in empty storefront, selling beer and numbers.
Old woman in black, black shawls,
folding chair squat on the doorstep,
hawk eyes, spits when she sees me.

I was a stranger there and young.
That world, that time, was past, already done,
new city coming into time, all new. But there it stood,
still tenanted and full, and I was there
just living there, though only passing through.

HART CRANE

So rash then reckless run to rant
bark after noon/ noun lost at sea
Cherroo/ Cherree
all up in my father's business
don't you know I must be?

Rough trade in Life Savers/ candy/ bars and
gerund a Gerald
a Geryon god. Mark the griffon in flight
through gaseous crepe hung low . . .

Ack ack the tune. Sing attar of burnt rose/ fire tong star-
starry eyes that penetrate/ detonate/ profligate ankles of rum,
of rum

de dum. My prodigal/
son/ my lovely
disgrace/ you say grace/ you say

ruin/ say lovely my dear say/ I'm done
lover mine say I'm not
going to make it/ this time.

NIJINSKY

The eagle takes the little birds
he takes their lives!
Their little lives—their all!

My God! Once I could leap and twirl
in air. Have you forgiven me?
A bird may hide in sky.
Oh no! In air
the eagle tears
at living flesh,
takes down what flies,
will take my life, my only life, my all.

I do not hate the eagle, God,
the bird is terrible and vast, a world, a great one
here among the small.
The great one takes the little worlds
to live in him. The great, the all.
But still—but still—the lives . . . they fall . . .

I am weeping as I write this.
I am weeping for the little birds.

ON A LINE FROM ROBINSON JEFFERS

And what of your promise? There was a thrill in the air
in the room around you when you moved or stood still, a crisp, charged
scent of ions—that was your promise. Laughter rang in the bar: your remark
was your promise. You could run with a bum leg, bet on the long shot, wake
up in a strange city and take out a loan. Women petted you; you lay back
casually on the velvet spread. Excitement preceded you, you owned what
you touched.

And what of your promise? Your cheekbone prefigured
sensibility, your arched eyebrow spoke wit. When the restaurant closed
you helped pull the doors tight, drew the blinds down low, and won money
at cards while you drank the host's liquor all night. Coming home at dawn
through night-wet alleys, we saw your shadow reflected in the deep shine
of asphalt. You drew a circle around yourself: the promise whispered you
to life, and glories hastened up, crackling like halos. The subway took you
whole, you invested tunnels with light. The city held you, and holding you,
held something of its own. The boy didn't want your wallet. He broke your
nose to spoil something perfect. Your face was better after, more manly,
people said.

And those nights in the cabin at the edge of the
meadow, your voice lifted over the stubble grass, speaking the song of
promise, singing the cry-out of acclaim. Heat lightning of your words,
sweet mountaintop of promise, intoxicating island Manhattan, streets of
promised wonder, honey hillsides of New Jersey, the museum café where a
lime seed is falling, rising, and falling between the ice cubes, sliding down
their surfaces, bubbles surrounding it, the light in the bubble surrounding
the seed in an effervescence of pressure. That was your promise, imminent,
an almost tangible light splitting you off from whatever could be enough,
from what was only you, one man; you sink, sustaining it.

I remember looking out from a departing airplane at
night, down upon the ancient city of Manhattan. Each light was a world

once promised to us. Stars and satellites shone above, their lights the same. Fire trailed from the fin of a plane. Buildings and neon, headlights, and the crackle of genius excitement below, all beautiful and dread. All were caught in a net being pulled up tight, whirled in a cluster like galaxies. The rock was ticking, full of time, the city lay far below and the night so wide. The city rose on its gleaming rock from a black ocean flecked with phosphorescence. Sheets of fire waved on the backs of the people; the closer they drew, the more their light increased. Blue flames fringed an outflung arm—fire shot from eyeholes—and around their heads were orange halos. The more they touched each other, the more brilliant the excited conversation, the higher the flames leapt between them. A band of people on a hillside sang with sexual energy and tried to make the wet grass burn. Tequila splashed in the field, and the field put it out. On a hill without light, the imagination grazed coolly. Inside, the cool dark of contemplation grew, and reached into the stone, the green wood, and the damp, fraying leaves.

Nothing turned back to the self, there was no stone where the wave might break. What we thought we lived for then seemed no more than a turbulence of the spirit, a crash of wills, contention giving off brief sparks of light. And I remembered the old poet counseled his sons: "Be in nothing so moderate as in love of man."

HOME FOOTAGE, 1970

This my witch's hand, sinistra,
that writes, and having writ rubs out
the script that would convict.
She it is silenced who in me set
electric fire, forged to fuse

dynamite, molotov, a missile in the night.
Pffft. We only lit
the curtains, and the armory stood.

Kaput all that.
It was half-livered revolution,
flower-heart wilting; we were lost
and found wanting, left needing
an author, a leader,
an army to make end befall.
No bullet-built world will bring to hand
the moment that refused its chance.

Still the image on the screen replays
the night, revises memory, rescinds the day.
Regard what mind preserved in lens,
put out the light to see
translucent image in the dark.

WILL SPRING EVER COME TO THE NORTH COUNTRY

No one on the road this morning. It's going to rain,
but not yet. Ice and black snow in the ditches
grainy with dirt, and gravel rolled up in little balls
here where the road turns under the hemlocks'
perpetual shade. Climbing the hill, my feet are heavy
and cold chews at my neck. Stiff from long winter,
I feel like a tractor straining to pull a stump.
Past the yellow house where no one comes or goes:
the man who lives there just got out of prison.
He stole from a club whose books he kept.
Three years: after paying his fines and his lawyers,
he got no profit from it. People don't think.
I fish a blue-and-silver can out of the brush,
as if I could save something from all this mess,
but it's breaking up, breaking down; mud
and the soup of time drip from the can,
shot through with holes, someone's target practice.
The trouble with time is we only see part of it. Leaning
over to pluck the can I twisted my knee and now
it won't unbend; I limp on for a few steps
until it loosens up. I'm going nowhere without these knees.
Not that I'm going anywhere—only home, to the woodstoves
burning up sunlight, the news crying tyranny.

PART THREE: *Deer in a Gated Park*

DEER IN A GATED PARK: A POEM IN FIVE PARTS

Wild gardens overlooked by night lights . . .
—Barbara Guest

1.

Bare woods' sky scrolled by snow. Grey car
under the window, scrolled by snow.
Beyond, three hundred acres of forest,
trees vertical and slant, straight lines
displacing perspective, rendering a grid,
a vista scrolled by snow.

The imagination wanders, lost in this
resurrected wilderness, second-growth forest,
hardwood and pine, staggered with stone walls
built by settlers: colonials self-transplanted,
sheep farmers and builders of barns.

Consider the organization of a tree
whose structure is mathematical—
a formula producing green.
Trees in woods producing trees,
aspiring upward, more vertical than lush,
overreaching themselves toward light.
How the world keeps finding its way back
to its first self, its one or two ideas:
root and seed. Leaves from leaves,
one code that raises woods from earth.

I pace the large, light-filled room
whose windows offer a landscape beyond touch,
a sense of cold awakened in the mind

by a view of snowy woods, dusk falling
into the spaces between things
and nesting there. In the room, a couch,
a red carpet woven with geometric figures,
a piano shining, mahogany and polished gleam,
white teeth of keys.

Beside the great stone hearth, beneath the mirrored
mantel, a stack of firewood with sharp edges,
logs freshly split, pale inside. Green wood.
The blaze in the great fireplace
licks up in little flames. I have built the fire
with wood piled in a box by my door,
left there at morning, with kindling of paper and sticks.

The piano is silent. I place my fingers on words,
counting weights and tones on a page.
The red carpet with figures that are geometric,
not representing nature, the faithful would say,
as if anything were not nature. All culture
and history gathers in this room: its glass and wood,
its cushions and table, the books with their marks
that stand for sounds and pictures in the mind,
and snow gently scrolling past high windows.

2.

The deer come at dusk and reach to the pine boughs.
Space opens around them with every step.
Imagining they are free,
they are free. Their part always
to step through the membrane, to reveal
there is no membrane, and no stepping through.

Tracks in fresh snow appear to lead
from one place to the next, as if to mark
a record of progress, a path occasioned
by circumstance and small moments of choice.
Accident of prints and accident of snow,
the sound of a plow scraping the road.

Once they would put a mark on the trees
that were tall and straight enough for ships' masts.
This meant the tree was owned by the king.
What we understood of tree then, how it appeared to us,
was changed. The element of comparison enters,
a judgment of ends, so that to see a tree now

is to imagine voyages:
wooden ships, timbers sawed to planks.
The king's table sanded to a gloss, moldings
embellished with carvings, all flourishes of rank
and circumstance, ceremony of majesty
that must be imagined before it can exist.
Mystery: that we had a king
and then did not. How he was imagined into being
and named sacred, a way of holding an idea
which might fall away if it were not held strongly
beyond mind, somehow appointed, ordained.

If a tree is property of the king,
we may assume a kingdom.
Stone walls, and sheep grazing cleared land.
The deer lie down in the pines,
or they wander under trees, inside a membrane
that moves with them, owning themselves.
We cannot feel what they know, the unbounded space
before each step. The king's deer
the peasant must not hunt on pain of death.

3.

Here is what I would say of the imagination:
that one thing disappears into another,
a lineage of similitude, repetition of ideas
reiterating the first act. Leaves made from leaves,
one code that raises forest out of earth. Yet we create
transformation, an alchemy of difference,
with our questions, inserting what is not
into the is—our ambition a secret charge.

But perhaps I have mistaken the question
and you are not looking for something made
and strange cornered in the mind, but rather
some lush utterance, a lyric unleash,
as in night gardens lit by desire,
fragrant strange flowers leaned down to whisper
secret fount. Something awaiting us,
some destiny given, to be discovered and entered whole.

Not this unmoving scene of woods
and scroll of snow, of which we make
what we will. I think you are wishing
for something that doesn't require making,
the sought-after thing the mind knows
as an animal knows, following a scent through woods,
through dark drawn on. What calls us out,
what we call after . . .

4.

Here a triptych of windows partitioned in squares,
glass and muntins, frame after frame repeating,
a grid laid over the woods, their wilds darkening beyond.
Dusk. I turn to the window, then to another window,
facing east, then north. I am beginning to see nothing
beyond this room with its high ceiling and the fire
burning in a grate, the tree consumed by air,
its sunlight heat released, rendering sap-juice
to blister and char. Crack and snap of branches
burning, and the roar of a car on the road below
breaking the dream. I did not see the cars
until it was dark and their lights flashed through the trees.
I was imagining wilderness, yet world was here,
its history and making. Abraham's sheep on the hillside,
the forests of Judah cut for ship's timbers.
Deer grazing on pine boughs as night falls. Snow
scrolling past darkening branches, blurred in snow light.

5.

Deer in a gated park, moving freely
inside the king's imagined wilderness.
Their tracks will melt. We read the past,
the way the deer has gone, not where it is going.

The table, a fire, a book of maps.
The map is drawn after the journey;
those otherwise conceived are useless,
fantastic with dragons, whirlpools, and djinns.

The question seemed to go on opening forever.
I could not find its dimensions.
Because I did not see the gate I wandered free
and made the world inside my mind.
The seed in the tree, the seed in the earth,
the tree inside the earth, and all the earth within.
One mystery of repeating: reiteration of form,
the moment made again, remade.

While the windows were transparent, made of light,
their spaces opening my vision, when the threshold
was invisible, I believed I was free. The world
continuous, a membrane interpenetrating, one realm
breathed into another. Then, gazing mastered space
though I looked from a frame made of wood
and glass, from a place built for shelter.

Prints mark the snow as snow falls to fill them,
and stone walls are rebuilt
though the sheep are gone, sold away
to other farms, their lineage continued,

their blood not lost though changed by time,
absorbed like salt in water, become real.

When the deer walk out of the frame
that holds our knowing, they are gone.
The grid dissolved, each kingdom perishing.
And still, sensing, we feel them ahead of us,
our subtle instruments, pulsed ahead into dark.
They send back signals too faint to read,
from worlds never reached by mind.

PART FOUR: *Garden Bench*

VIEW THROUGH APERTURES

I refresh my mind by looking through the door
that opens to another room beyond. I'm lying on a sofa
as I look across into the next room, which is empty,
which makes the view restful.

I lie on the sofa, which is too narrow really for comfort,
balanced with one foot on the floor as if I might get up
and walk away. But for now I lie back
and gaze into the empty space,
the white walls and open doorway just beyond.
I notice a small insect, some gnat or fly,
floating in the air, touching nothing, and this is restful.

When we come to the end of our wanting,
it will be like this. The eye traveling in white air,
and the pale glow of the window diffusing,
not broadcasting, daylight.

When the argument ends and the office closes
and everyone goes home to bed, it will be like this.
Not caring so much if things went our way.
After so much trouble,

not really minding. Just walking into the house
and listening. No one would be there.
Drinking a glass of water in the kitchen
and going straight upstairs.

When you are turning you may be retracing, repeating your gaze across space, where you were then in time. Where you were then must be reviewed, overseen, revealed, or stepped through again. In time. Discovering then another time and space, as over your shoulder both would be reversed, unwound. So you must turn and reiterate point of view; then you will see what you approached from that aspect that was hidden on your approach,

self-obscured, as it were. Because every outlook has a reverse, to and fro making one flip-flap. Depending on direction. When you are turning you may graze the outline of an image, reshape it perhaps, refined, made less by touch, as stone is worn, the grindstone ground by centuries' turning, by dust and water smoothed to small. So when you are turning you might reconsider and be wise. New prospect is perspective and may yield revision. You may yield;

the energy of turning is not hard though we resist. In turning you must renegotiate terrain; you will be caught off-center, showing your flank, not quite retreating nor yet regrouped; still and all you present a wider target. You do not yet quite represent. Neither will you be holding fortifications, ground dug in with fortitude. Expand your outlook, then; to turn requires space. You won't be rooted yet, or pent. Repent. To turn implies surprise. You can't be sure of what's behind you that is appearing now before you, as in turning toward you must always turn away.

The screw buries itself in the frame. Turning toward what you have left behind, you may find yourself come round full circle, and then what has happened? This getting nowhere, as turntable, scratch of stylus, inscribes return. I'm dizzy now, I feel a little sick, confused, spun round. Once I was headed somewhere, then a doubt or a temptation stopped me, and I turned aside. Forgetting my keys, I turned back to the house. I turned back when I remembered forgetting.

Having briefly forgotten, I returned remembering. Turn here: a question of precision: to find the street, turn right, which does not mean to say to turn correctly. Find the mailbox, the driveway, the door. Turn in. Turn the key, turn the knob, turn on lights, turn down the bed, turn back the clock, turn off the light, turn in, turn over in bed, kiss someone goodnight, la la. But no, you have, or you may have, turned unaccountably into something strange, say a demon, or a vapor no one would kiss. Perhaps a mere ether wafted along the wall, searching a way out into the trees. Desperate, disparate, diasporite. So, when you are turning you are disoriented and dismay may dismiss you; you may

be deranged, not able to recant, to remember it's your turn to take out the trash, which is past now, due to be buried or burned. Redeem the empty, call breath back from vows. For now it's late, the order is written, the gates are closing, the horn is blown, the letter has gone out with no return address.

What I'm saying is that one day the future will end, where you will possess only the past, and you will stand as it is written to make account, left without recourse, arrested, at rest in yourself, where you have always been.

HORSE

The horse stood alone in a pasture; the grass was high. The horse's heart was empty. The deep sameness of things held her peacefully. Because the grass was high, she seemed to rise from the pasture, a figure floating in green, the high grass reiterating her motion as she passed. I thought the horse was lonely and I grieved. The horse became my sorrow, all the grief I could ever know or bear, and in the pasture there was no more horse, no grass; the semblance of animal haunted the day like an erasure on a page, like mist rising in figured shapes. The deep similarity of the world to itself, the sameness of things, reverberated. Until I became, myself, the horse in the pasture, until my mind will be still with a loneliness that is empty of other worlds, until my mind is still and the grass overtakes me.

PRIVATE BEACH

At the sea place, a deep privacy: a scene, or a way of speaking without membranes. We loitered there, winding down the shaded walk overgrown with honeysuckle, ivory horns with their sweet nectar covering under-odor of rot, and skunks who love-nest under the boards. Light separated the spindles of the railing, giving each its own shadow, and the many shadows of perfect strangers on the beach overlapped and mingled in slow time, astronomical hours, as the tide covered and uncovered rocks and sand, shells, broken crockery, shoe leather, clay pipes, and rusted iron. The deep privacy of these things, glimpsed for a few hours between the sea's long movements, their secret world revealed, then gone.

I walked with the old woman, my hostess' neighbor, an elegant beauty who moved slowly on bandaged feet. A young man in yellow trousers spoke to us from a porch. He had a damaged mind, and his hair grew up like sea grass in clumps rich and odd; he traveled with his mother, he spoke of her, and the damaged voice formed perfectly, with too much care, careful sentences, as if everything were strange or new. He seemed to listen to himself as he spoke. As if speaking beyond us. We answered briefly and moved away. And the woman with the pale olive skin, the aged beauty, the clear-voiced woman whose feet were wound in bandages turned her head to me, with the slightest turning, saying: What at first seems interesting is not of interest in the end. Thinnest air. What you call novelty is an old story to me. I might stop to answer a stranger, feeling idle or kind, but never hoping to learn about life.

I mean to say, she said, I've already read a book.

She let her feet down into the water; a loose tendril of gauze floated like purest seaweed at her ankle. The water was rising then and met her, though this meant nothing. I scratched up a shell with my toes. The tide pools filled, making widening pools scattered across the brown continents of sand banks. We turned our backs on the others, leaned closer to make a space for the moment to occur, and that deep privacy to reveal itself, as it would reveal, yet remain private. The young man leaned on the railing above us, looking out far, not banished, less than banished, merely contained by our turning away, held within himself. Waves splashed the wooden steps softly, softly met and refused, the constant movement of cloud shadows, change of colors, the yellow trousers bright and singular. Our turning away left him a place to stand and search inside himself, a flash of thought, but who could know it, how follow the private reaches of a damaged mind wandering in the sheltered space of afternoon, returned again on itself?

The color of the beach was yellow, an aura of yellow, a wash on the air. The mother came out to call her son. The boy—the man—looked up. I ran my fingers along the edge of the stair. I thought of yesterday's perfect child who played with the sand that would not stick together to make towers, who packed it and packed it, and carried pails of water, wearing a scar of seaweed across his chest. How he balanced patiently with grace inside himself, how he ran to us in nouns and verbs, and ran away again and stayed inside himself, not seeing himself, leaning to nothing.

JACKASS ANGELS

The storm now icing over, cars spin out on Route Six,
power lines snap and flail in north winds.
I drove for hours in a fugue; the snow blew straight
across the highway, and the road kept appearing
and disappearing ahead of me—no lanes,
and those white veils ghosted up before the headlights.
It was some trick, I decided, a dream of worlds conflated,
and I kept driving as if I could see it all clearly
ahead of me, though my passage was slow,
and the cars were all creeping along like dromedaries,
and now and then I'd pass one that had slid off the side,
and landed upright in a ditch, the passengers
wiping peepholes in vapored windows,
looking stunned and happy after such a twirl.
Radio sputtering weather delays: St. Peter's
Shepherds and Angels rehearsal canceled,
the Blue Christmas Singles Party postponed.
Headed into a dead zone then, the voices went out,
drowned in static, and there was nothing to advise me,
but inside my mind I was traveling
into the power that was not my power, falling inward,
down to point zero, where everything ends
and begins again. I was transparent, and alone
in the way of eternity as I understood it then,
outside myself, and when I got to town all the lights
were out. I inched my car down the one street,
steering past dark storefronts to find the one place open,
where I ordered a curry and an Indian beer. Two men
who watched me walk in floated down from the bar,
lighting at my table, one on either side, as if to continue

a discussion interrupted only moments before.
One was short, with slicked-back hair and jackal eyes;
he said he was an investment banker.
He was an investment banker like I'm an opera star,
and his friend, who'd said nothing, just nodded,
and drummed his fingers on the table.
Are you a writer, he asked as if fortune-telling,
and I said *yes*. A fair guess in this town.
Are you a famous writer? he pressed his luck,
and I said *no*. He recognized me from somewhere,
they always do, these jackass angels,
junior messengers of the lower orders;
they've looked you up and already know everything,
but sometimes they like to mess with you,
showing off, or maybe just bored between assignments.
The "banker" was eating food from my plate
with his fingers, and his friend ordered beers;
it was clear it was all on my bill, and that was fine,
the night was young. They were headed out to God
knows where, and they asked would I come
with them, but I know that while a jackass angel
can get you to heaven as well as any other, it won't be pretty,
it will involve ridiculous and unnecessary compromise,
and awkward adventures in unseemly venues,
and I'd just driven through a blizzard to get there, so no.
I paid and buttoned up my coat, wrapped scarves at the door;
they flanked me gently, like wings.
Oh, the night was so cold, and the street gone quiet.
The town felt holy with the snow falling heavy in the street,
and falling into the black water of the harbor,
and on all the houses with candles in their windows,
and my feet leaving big ghostly prints as I walked

back to my room. They didn't stay with me for long,
they were disheartened for maybe a moment,
then bummed a couple of cigarettes (then, thinking it over,
took a couple more without asking) and wandered off
up the street with the red sparks pulsing at their lips
like fireflies. I used to say I'd go anywhere any time
any angel asked, but you don't have to
take them so seriously, you don't have to follow them
into the night, or wrestle them for a blessing,
just laugh and say *not this time,* and they'll let you go.
And sometimes they'll tell you their names:
Tom. Brian.

AFTER PESSOA

It is not yet autumn, but late summer here. The leaves are still green and a little tired, draped like fabric on the small trees that edge the parking lot. The cool of morning comes ahead of the midday heat, which is brief now. The air is thin and can't hold much warmth, and when the sun goes a chill bores through space and settles into bodies. Sounds travel quickly in the thin air. They are sharp and do not blend into one another. A door snaps shut twice: excellent staccato. Out in the dooryard a woman laughs. Who spoke before? Quick steps on gravel punctuating every passage, every coming and going. In a few weeks it will be fall. We are preparing for things disappearing, the birds and flowers, then the leaves, and then the light. For now summer lingers. Comes some cry in the air and I feel a surge of unease, my heart bracing for the departures. The indifference of their vanishing. Then the twilight lowers and the walls drink their own shadows. A lighted window throws a rectangle of white on the ground: an antishadow. Soon we will be carving up the dark with lamps.

Days I walk the streets of this small city among familiar scenes, things growing old before my gaze. A wooden gate hanging loose. A sign in a café window bearing a tired promise of beach holidays. I remember when these were new. The hand I put forward to push open a shop door shows its sinews in the hard light, the skin crossed with fine lines, alluvial. How have I lived so long? It seems only days since I was a child. These streets are layered with memory. I keep my eyes down as I walk—I might burn a passerby with my gaze.

I buy a paper at the little store. How many papers, how many yesterdays' news? Summer is passing. I rehearse these words as if I might believe them, but I haven't gotten there yet. The season turns, the light goes down. Nothing will last. The yellow bicycle leaned against a wall in the alley behind the offices. The crab apple with its hard orange fruit, sour and bright, its limbs balancing, leaning into the sun. A young woman showing off a new belt, a present from a man, to a friend on the sidewalk. Her shoes' shiny patent sparking when she walks. They are gone; no trace of them remains. The white stripes of the crosswalk, the grand clock in the Town Hall tower, vanished, forgotten. The man in the apartment upstairs has a wife and a lover, both beautiful. He sits up all night with his novel, writing his mind into the world, as if this could undo time. We are dedicated, each in our way, to undoing time. But it is all ended: whoever loved or was loved, whatever work was done or left undone; the night is coming, none of this can stay. The water in a cup, lying so still, and the black tarp stretched over the truck bed, huffing lightly in wind. And now the reflections in the still water of the pond, light multiplied, the world constellated in shadowy images, and the coat hung on a hook by the door for coming and going, how everything relies on everything else, and nothing at the center to hold. Sweep away the house and there is no door, no meaning for the idea of door, no going out or coming in, no one to wear a coat.

Take away the sky, no light or wind. And it is gone. Our world is gone. Infinity swallows time: impossible. But who is saying this—what mind or eye imagines a witness, a place from which to behold the nothing that opens inside each mind, though we can never see it, only feel the dark wing brush and dip? And so we start and turn and lie awake with dread beating on our lips, and it is never there, always just beyond, and were we ever to reach it we would not be. We are always going. And beyond, past every journey, the ancient, awful silence of the universe, which does not know time or space, where there is nothing, and always is a grim and cheerless word. And yet it is summer here, the air is soft with salt air and late flowers, and in the dooryard a woman laughs.

THE VALUE OF POETRY

Simonides was the first poet to charge money for his verses. Accused of avarice, he remained unmoved. Once after a dinner, the patron for whom he had written an ode refused to pay the agreed-on price. Angry, Simonides stormed out of the feast. Moments later an earthquake struck, killing everyone in the building. The bodies were broken and maimed beyond recognition, but Simonides, still holding the poem he had written, was able to identify each of them according to where the person had been seated, which was meticulously catalogued in his lines.

Once Simonides was walking by the seashore on the eve of departure for an ocean journey when he came upon a corpse the waves had cast up, which he did not hesitate to bury, and, being Greek and a poet, he wrote a poem as epitaph for the stranger. That night the dead man appeared to him in a dream and warned him not to sail in the morning. Simonides relayed this omen to his fellow travelers, who ignored him. They set out and all were shipwrecked. Simonides alone was saved.

It avails one so to bury the dead, and to raise up monuments in perishing words for the stranger cast up on shore. It is also wise to leave the party when you are no longer welcome.

WE WILL BE TWO

We will be two horses in a field,
a mild morning in early winter,
light traffic moving below the hill
in the distance, not troubling the air.

Headlights ghost the snowfields:
neighbors driving their children to school,
and going on to work, and we stand,
two horses breathing steam.

The field is wide, cut by a little stream
that runs downhill into woods
with a view of mountains beyond.
The view drops off over hillsides,

and light flows evenly
across the space between. The hour passes,
traffic ceases, and we stand there quiet
as day brightens, and patches of green

begin to appear where the snow melts away.
We bend our heads to the grass to graze
as sun moves over our bodies,
warming our heavy coats, down to muscle,

then bone; we move easily then,
deep inside the world,
all snow and mountain here,
all field and wood beyond.

Where we stand will be the center,
time moving through us as light.
We will be two horses in a field,
The earth rolls away where we stand,
all snow and mountain here,
all field and wood beyond.
Where we stand will be the center,
time moving through us as light.

HUM

first summer sleep floats among mountains rising
and falling slides along surface of water and down
long valleys enters by windows floats there grazing
the ceiling the sky's imagining pauses over you hovers
there enters your body you are this moment all world
alive incarnate you are the aggregate sum total of
sense and want self-moored below dreaming awake
to wave of dune grass airplane in black sky skunk
passing under the window redolent funk of night
dark lit with animal heat the hum the sway and the
hollow your body graves in the bed how your hungers
call out like commands from the earth first urge first
summer sleep is ten thousand wakenings each breath
a green world flutter of wing hill of grass and what
might be the heart unsure still loyal to the want that
calls itself being seduced by tangled brush and vine
the broken stump of the cherry tree the wind brought
down that was another time and place the hollow
the woodchuck dug under its roots long dead he lies
inside his winter sleep each breath releases air and
calls air back to fill an emptiness with all that breath
implies the drift above around and through the self
and the "I" tells the "you" *I am sleeping* chooses and
unchooses again to enter the resting form will not
cease considering will not resolve to descend or to
remain a soul beyond this blood this ether you know
is yours torrid salt-rich if the heart if the breath bring
it freshening newly made of dandelion and dust the
red ants challenging the chafed terrain first summer
sleep forgets that if you leave this body you may

never lift the clump of grass left by the mower hold
it in hand to scatter may not witness the crab apple
flinging blossoms or the blackbirds who come at once
to the earth in company and depart the earth at once
in company showing no reason for going or coming
first summer sleep forsakes the covenant it falls lush
and faithless wanting everything still more the stillness
between each breath the heart's hesitation before
beating and all the while the sweet air offering all
it cannot speak or intend but if the soul once relents
to taste and feel the weight of every striving leaf and
bone of being it is in the air a drift like maple key
spun down reluctant exuberant air invisible as
the moment is invisible you live here

GARDEN BENCH

Late August flickers,
the sultry and the gleam.
Brief mountain summer.
The garden bench pale under porch lights,
a silk current shines through
its iron scrolls, and feels its way
among the branches and leaves.
The garden sleeps
and night swims in, filling every form.
Larvae spun into chrysalides.
The bark beetle chewing.

Night is a place. We enter it.
Large, with no edges, it has curved on itself,
an inside with no outside. I can put my hand
through it without tearing. It moves
through me too, though it is everywhere.

Some bread and cheese,
a glass of water. Are you lonely here?
It's so much more than that. The great mass
of the maple tree, standing in the yard,
fifty years growing, half of it underground.
Each branch a root. Crown in the sky.
Close your eyes, let it raise you.
If I were that.

Or a stone
broken from the ledge, lying among leaves.
What do you call a broken stone? A stone.
Always complete.
A door, moved by a handle back and forth,
one arc governed by a hinge,
the plane of the door shuttering light,
opening and closing space.

How times comes and goes in things.
An old pot holding water.
Or a moth the porch light baffled.
A work glove left in the grass. Or a nail,
driven to its limit, tight inside the wood.
Holding it, held.

ACKNOWLEDGMENTS

Grateful acknowledgment is made to the editors of the magazines and presses where the following poems (sometimes in earlier versions) were published:
"Deer in a Gated Park" appeared in *Terrain*.
"Hart Crane" appeared in *RHINO*.
"Horse" originally appeared in *Agni* and was later published in my chapbook *Gnomon*, from Jacar Press.

Blessings: Orhan Pamuk, Tomas Transtromer, Frank O'Hara, Hart Crane, Vaslov Nijinsky, Robinson Jeffers, Barbara Guest, Fernando Pessoa, Simonides, Walt Whitman, Gerard Manley Hopkins.

Many thanks to Mark Cox, John Donaghy, and David Wojahn for help with the work in progress.

I am thankful for residencies at the MacDowell Colony and Arteles Creative Center, where some of these poems began.

And in grateful memory of Jon Tribble.

OTHER BOOKS IN THE CRAB ORCHARD SERIES IN POETRY

The Flesh Between Us
Tory Adkisson

Muse
Susan Aizenberg

Millennial Teeth
Dan Albergotti

Hijra
Hala Alyan

Instructions, Abject & Fuming
Julianna Baggott

Lizzie Borden in Love: Poems in Women's Voices
Julianna Baggott

This Country of Mothers
Julianna Baggott

The Black Ocean
Brian Barker

Vanishing Acts
Brian Barker

Objects of Hunger
E. C. Belli

Nostalgia for a World Where We Can Live
Monica Berlin

The Sphere of Birds
Ciaran Berry

White Summer
Joelle Biele

Gold Bee
Bruce Bond

Rookery
Traci Brimhall

USA-1000
Sass Brown

The Gospel according to Wild Indigo
Cyrus Cassells

In Search of the Great Dead
Richard Cecil

Twenty First Century Blues
Richard Cecil

Circle
Victoria Chang

Errata
Lisa Fay Coutley

Salt Moon
Noel Crook

Consolation Miracle
Chad Davidson

From the Fire Hills
Chad Davidson

The Last Predicta
Chad Davidson

Unearth
Chad Davidson

Furious Lullaby
Oliver de la Paz

Names above Houses
Oliver de la Paz

Dots & Dashes
Jehanne Dubrow

The Star-Spangled Banner
Denise Duhamel

Smith Blue
Camille T. Dungy

Seam
Tarfia Faizullah

Beautiful Trouble
Amy Fleury

Sympathetic Magic
Amy Fleury

Egg Island Almanac
Brendan Galvin

Soluble Fish
Mary Jo Firth Gillett

Pelican Tracks
Elton Glaser

Winter Amnesties
Elton Glaser

Strange Land
Todd Hearon

Burn
Sara Henning

View from True North
Sara Henning

Always Danger
David Hernandez

Heavenly Bodies
Cynthia Huntington

Terra Nova
Cynthia Huntington

Maps for Migrants and Ghosts
Luisa A. Igloria

Zion
TJ Jarrett

Red Clay Suite
Honorée Fanonne Jeffers

Fabulae
Joy Katz

Cinema Muto
Jesse Lee Kercheval

Train to Agra
Vandana Khanna

The Primitive Observatory
Gregory Kimbrell

If No Moon
Moira Linehan

Incarnate Grace
Moira Linehan

For Dust Thou Art
Timothy Liu

Strange Valentine
A. Loudermilk

Dark Alphabet
Jennifer Maier

Lacemakers
Claire McQuerry

Tongue Lyre
Tyler Mills

Oblivio Gate
Sean Nevin

Holding Everything Down
William Notter

The Kitchen of Small Hours
Derek N. Otsuji

American Flamingo
Greg Pape

Crossroads and Unholy Water
Marilene Phipps

Birthmark
Jon Pineda

Fieldglass
Catherine Pond

No Acute Distress
Jennifer Richter

Threshold
Jennifer Richter

On the Cusp of a Dangerous Year
Lee Ann Roripaugh

Year of the Snake
Lee Ann Roripaugh

Misery Prefigured
J. Allyn Rosser

Into Each Room We Enter without Knowing
Charif Shanahan

In the Absence of Clocks
Jacob Shores-Arguello

Glaciology
Jeffrey Skinner

Roam
Susan B. A. Somers-Willett

The Laughter of Adam and Eve
Jason Sommer

Hinge
Molly Spencer

Huang Po and the Dimensions of Love
Wally Swist

Persephone in America
Alison Townsend

Spitting Image
Kara van de Graaf

Becoming Ebony
Patricia Jabbeh Wesley

Even the Dark
Leslie Williams

The River Where You Forgot My Name
Corrie Williamson

All the Great Territories
Matthew Wimberley

Abide
Jake Adam York

A Murmuration of Starlings
Jake Adam York

Persons Unknown
Jake Adam York